Biden's Autumn: Trump & the Republican's Fall

by Zeek Ethan Keekee

©July 2020

"Some people cause happiness wherever they go;
some whenever they go."
-Oscar Wilde

———

We are doing a great job. This is a key focal point, and we must be careful to not become overly negative. Our purpose is not to waste time and words worshiping politicians or fretting over things that are out of our control. Worshiping politicians is not on our agenda.

Investing in wise uses of time leads us to seek to be informed. Reading and trying to help others to read and think clearly is a priority in our lives. Therefore, to put it simply, we keep a positive attitude—an attitude of gratitude. Avoiding impurity, we acknowledge that sarcasm is the language of the devil.

In very deed we go forward bravely, fearing no toil nor labor of mind or body. Seeking to pass the rest of our days in a spirit of humility, we observe that the wise American of Yesterday was not scared of good work. The country of present-day Americans and the knowledgeable individual will continue to work for wisdom, looking at all angles and perspectives, not jumping to conclusions and keeping unnecessary emotion out of the equation. Those seeking to improve will strive for charitable activity and to have the mind of wisdom in their hearts and souls. Tamping down foolishness, striving for charity, and battling to forgive and to be forgiven is the American way. That is the truth.

Many rational beings could see Trump's Fall and Biden's Autumn coming from a long way off. Those who beheld the situation by divine revelation knew wars and plagues were soon coming to pass. The impending divisions, contentions, lasciviousness, whoredoms, vanity, foolishness, murder, and the destruction of the family was not only the result of the presidential elections but also of human freedom in a broader context. Opposites and the law of opposition is the price we pay for freedom of will. Free to choose the good or the evil, each individual and nation must make their own decisions.

An examination of the past reveals many righteous and fine deeds done by ourselves and others. Even a brief examination reveals the proper thing for the proper reason was accomplished in many instances. Since the fall or otherwise, looking back at pointed conversations and communication reveals good uses of money, the proper labeling of truths and falsehoods, and insightful analysis of political conditions.

Learning to handle money, deflation, inflation, and stagflation came to pass.

Additionally, contrite spirits detected those who called evil "good." Others went on to call good "evil," and they too were detected.

Many good and worthwhile things happened during the times of Trump & Biden. A level of cleanliness associated with Covid disease-distancing also brought about an increase of scripture reading. This brought about an increase of righteousness, an increase that was not easy to maintain as the pull of the world was strong. And the weakness of fallen humans was understood and known. Therefore, forgiveness transpired and continues. Even though future opportunities to read scripture are lost by the negligent when the threat of death and destruction seems to relinquish its grasp, extreme circumstances may humble and correct the decaying few.

By prophecy we know the personification of the Spirit of truth will arrive on the face of the earth. He will live among his people. The thoughts and intents of the hearts of men will be spoken from the housetops. At that time—at the formal arrival of God in the Spirit and in the resurrected flesh— Trump and Biden will be the least of anyone's concerns. The Lord of Knowledge will, at one time or another, judge all men according to their works, according to the desires of their hearts. And we will be heartily glad that we sought the best books, the best thoughts, the best deeds, the best lifestyles, and the best motivations.

Judging souls is not within everyone's capability. But judging cause-and-effects is truly everyone's duty. This means analyzing what shall result from any given thought, action, or set of thoughts and actions. It is wisdom always to ask, "Where will this lead and what shall be the result?" The Trump worshipper and the Biden sympathizer knows that Entertainment is not our God, even if they choose death in its various forms.

To not read, to be illiterate, is to fight against America. To not read is to die. Knowledge must be obtained. Now is the time to make the journey to the straight and narrow path of righteousness. The broad way of wickedness can never be a happy way. Holiness is the only safe road to travel. If we can find it, we must help others.

"I may not walk the straight and narrow, but I sure as heck cross it as often as I can." Let this be our motto for now if we cannot do better. Let the worship of money come to an end. Let the mass media's worship of politicians come to an end.

Biden and Trump pass away like smoke in the wind, like the blossoms of a thistle in the breeze, like dry corns stalks trodden upon by the manure-caked hooves of cattle. We bid them farewell. We bid them peace. And when all is measured in the balance, it will be seen that these things were for our experience and consideration and, thus, for our benefit.

Section 1

Ignorance is Our Enemy:

Foundational Structures

-

To appreciate Biden's Autumn / Trump & the Republican's Fall, it behooves us to remind ourselves that a particular portion of the population strives to find the truth and to discover what is going on. There are those who appreciate knowledge of things as they are, as they were, and as they will be. Americans are doing a great job in many things.

The past can illuminate and offer insights into the future and the present. Distilling the past into a few words is the task of the first section of this book. Furthermore, the important foundation and history of God-fearing pilgrims and pioneer ancestors who sacrificed their comfort and lives to build and preserve this great nation is a portion of the past to which the rising generations need to be exposed. In some instances, we need to understand the past in order to understand the present.

We are successfully helping the poor and ignorant classes of people to deliver themselves from evil. At the same time, there has been a terrible decline in reading with the advent of the cell phone and other distractions. However, we continue to help the poor and ignorant masses and classes. When few continue to seek education, we must consider our ways.

Military personnel across the planet risk their lives and ours for money, adventure, duty, and for lack of better ideas. Teachers go into the classroom to risk their lives for money and to help kids. Politicians do the same. If we were to include the whole story and paint the entire picture of what is going on in America, libraries and museums would be filled with the miracles being worked. The picture would show most people are trying to do the right thing, and there is every good reason to keep hope. As reading Americans, we cross the straight and narrow as often as we can. That is sufficient to move forward without fear, bravely helping ourselves and our neighbors to improve.

Examples of History Repeating Itself

&

Definitions:

A-

Absolutism:

Political absolutism: Some of the Caesars of the Roman Empire tried to trace their lineage to deities and wanted to be deified by their subjects. King Henry 8th of England, who declared himself above the control of the Church, had wives and advisors killed, had people call him "your majesty," believed that he ruled by divine right. Also, Louis 16th of France, James 1st of England as well as several popes and Pharaohs declared they ruled by "divine right."

Religious absolutism: Catholic Church had nearly absolute control during medieval times because the church and state were almost the same. Popes declared the Church was above any earthly power, not merely regarding lawful purposes, but regarding whatever means necessary to attain control. Popes were purported to be infallible. The church was declared perfect and any attempts to change it were considered blasphemous and heretical, those who tried were subject to torture, even burning at the stake in extreme cases. Heretics were likened to Satan; demons and witches to control any changes and challenges to the power of the leaders. What came to be labeled through time as the "Spanish Inquisition" killed hundreds and caused paranoia for the whole country.

Adams, John: (1735-1826) was 2nd US president. Wife was Abigail. He was a strong advocate of natural rights which were God-given, thought men were not perfect but with proper institutions could become decent. Thought that paper laws and written constitutions were not merely creations of men, though not necessarily given by the God of FRICAW (facts, reality, impartiality, compassion, action, and wisdom). Adams favored a militant stance against Great Britain. He and Jefferson became friends and died on the same day. It is thought that John Adams had an I.Q. of about 155. John Quincy Adams (6th President) was their son, had an I.Q. of about 165.

ADHD: attention deficit hyperactivity disorder. Symptoms of ADHD: misdirected enthusiasm, impatient, poor mental organization, reckless physical organization, trouble with self-control, physically impulsive, not sustaining a job through thick and thin, difficulty concentrating *even on things of interest* such as video games, attracted to a lot of external things at the same time or in quick succession, accident prone, unchecked comments, late and distracted, trouble managing money, impulsive purchases, gambling. Causes of ADHD: Lack of discipline, bad parenting, immaturity, physiological deformity, and too much desire. Remedy: jogging, as much as ten miles a day.

Ad hominem: translates from Latin as "to the man;" appealing to the feelings or prejudices rather than intellect; attacking character rather than thoughts or opinions. Attack on the person rather than the argument, issue, or case. "The lawyer admonished the jurors to not be duped by the defense's ad hominem attack."

Adult Development: Advancement and progress through these stages comes through experiencing and working through conflict. (Huyck, Margret H. and William J. Hoyer. 1982. *Adult Development and Aging. Belmont*, Ca. Wadsworth Publishing.)

Erickson's Stages:

1) Basic trust and mistrust: Ages 0-1

2) Autonomy versus doubt: Ages 2-3

3) Quick versus slow: Ages 3-6

4) Work versus inferiority: Ages 6-12

5) Ego identity versus role diffusion: overcoming role confusion and establishing a sense of soul identity, finding body and mind limits and discovering patterns and schemas to adopt and act upon to make life easier and decision-making quicker. Ages: adolescence

6) Intimacy versus isolation: Ages: 20-30

7) Generosity versus stagnation: overcoming stagnation and establishing a sense of generosity by parenting, mentoring, creating, contributing. Ages: middle age

8) Soul integrity versus despair: overcoming despair and establishing a sense of integrity. Favorable

outcomes include renunciation of despair and developing wisdom and a positive attitude.

Adversary, Satan: selfishness at the End of its Journey. Adversary of mankind and God as a being who devotes time to causing injustice, doing unmerciful deeds, misusing power, and being dishonest. Adversary (Hassatan) means 'nuisance' in Hebrew scripture; influenced by pagan ideas such as Manicheism. In Revelation (or John's Apocalypse), Satan is a cosmic figure or infinite entity in the form of a real person and a final adversary for God in end times and always.

Advertising: A form of propaganda used to trick people into buying things they otherwise might not want or need. Political advertising is the art of selling people ideas and getting them to support politicians who may not have their best interests at heart. Advertising could be thought of as applied-psychology, it works by circumventing our conscious reasoning processes in order to manipulate the emotions and unconscious amygdala-triggered reactions (Frances, p. 165-166).

Advertising turned into a force acting on the public mind so successfully that it now serves to propel every kind of purpose, dogma, political and private ambition, and hence advertising with its peculiar status as approved deceit and temptation is not always challenged. Since technology drives production, new appetites as well as old must be kept at a high level, and in effect rich and poor must be made to live with the sense of continual deprivation. There are always new necessities and therefore perpetual indebtedness. "The standard of living" or conspicuous consumption of the rich became an agent of oppression. (Barzun, J. 2000.

Decadence: 500 Years of Western Cultural Life – 1500 to the Present. New York: Harper Collins, p. 602, 778.)

Emotional, intuitive, System 1—very common, dominates: probably 95% of ads, lots of hype, "legal deception and lying." Examples: vitamins promising to transform your life, beer will make you handy with the opposite gender, Dodge Ram trucks suggest big tough indestructibility or Jaguar SUVs are fast conferring up-scale status.

Rational, informative, System 2—quite rare: lists benefits and limitations with side effects, rational and scientific. Examples: some medical ads without hype or excessive emotion although tinged with legalese. Reviews in Consumer Reports, some articles in Car & Driver, medical reports such as PDR, studies using double blind tests.

Advertising that works on fear: You are too thin, too fat, too ugly, are not pretty enough, not strong enough, are not clean enough, have bad breath, teeth are yellow, your car is old and unreliable, you are too white, black, Latino, an immigrant, deplorable, low class, high class, old, young, dumb, ignorant, not refined, have bad hair, skin, nails, and out of it, etc.

Political ads often use fear of nationalism, socialism, communism, conspiracies, the unwashed other, immigrants, Muslims, etc, to get votes for the party who will solve all problems. Mencken's "goblin chasers," inventing false dilemmas.

<u>**Ages of History**</u>: labeled for academic testing and categorical convenience; language limitations and lack of firsthand knowledge leaves much to the imagination.

Paleolithic: ~100,000 BC to 13,000 BC. Primitive stone tools possible. Prior to this, fragments of other planets could have combined to form earth, on which dinosaurs may have lived. Defining the term "earth" can be a stumbling block to understanding.

Civilizations: ~12,000 BC to 8000 BC Gobekli Tepe temple emerged, Jericho town of thousands about 8500 BC. Records and guesses concerning communities begin with "the emergence of towns, when there is enough agricultural surplus and food that humans can specialize in one job such as iron makers, potters, farmers."

Pre-history: not much writing to be found before 3500 BC.

Copper Age: ~3500 BC, the name came from Cyprus, early copper manufacturing. Began about 2400 BC in Mesopotamia, later about 1200 BC in Palestine.

Bronze Age: writings from 3300 BC to 1200 BC in Mesopotamia and Egypt, in Americas as early as 3000 BC. In England, Stonehenge marked a move to the Bronze Age. Remains were found of a Bronze Age village that was built on stilts called "Musk Farm." City in Austria had glass beads and other glass. Bronze was 85% copper and 15% tin, helped to raise enough crops to provide food surpluses so some could be craftsmen and could trade.

Iron Age: ~1300 BC.

Axial Age: 600 BC. Zoroaster (1200 BC); time when major world religions and philosophies were possibly recorded including Buddhism, Hebrew prophets, Hinduism, Daoism, democracy of Solon.

Dark Ages: 410 AD to 1000 AD. After Vandals sacked Rome in 410 AD, little learning or literacy, library destroyed at Alexandria by Vandals, Mongols. Most citizens and most priests were illiterate, no books, only a few scrolls and parchments.

Middle Ages: 467 AD to 1454 AD. The fall of the Roman Empire in the West to the fall of Constantinople in 1454 AD.

Renaissance: 1300 AD to 1500 AD. Rebirth of learning especially in arts. Started in Florence, Italy with Dante, Michelangelo, Leonardo da Vinci, Machiavelli, Cervantes.

Reformation: 1500 AD to 1660 AD. This time period is often defined from the printing press (1450 AD) to the deaths of Luther and Calvin; both religious and political upheavals.

Age of Reason and Enlightenment: 17th century. Locke, Newton, Descartes, Hume, Kant, Voltaire, Jefferson, Franklin, Hutcheson, Adam Smith, Thomas Paine. Reason and science emerged. Kings such as Louis 16th and Henry 8th not of divine right; parliaments increased voice of the people.

Age of Ideology: 1800 AD to 1900 AD. Evolution, nationalism, communism, democracy, socialism, empire building, taking enlightenment to the savages. Joseph Smith, Brigham Young, Wilford Woodruff, Claude Monet, Tchaikovsky, Thomas Hardy, Karl Marx.

Age of Analysis: 1900 AD to 1999 AD. Deconstruction, Derrida, WWI, Hitler, Churchill, WWII, Korean War, Vietnam, Afghanistan, Iraq war efforts to control oil. George 5th, George 6th, Reagan, Bush, Clinton, Heber J. Grant, David O. McKay, Harold B. Lee, Howard W. Hunter.

Age of the Screen: 2000 AD to present. iPhones, computers, YouTube, Netflix, Zoom meetings, Facebook, widespread internet, ChatGPT, Covid-19; Trump, Biden, Victoria, Charles III, Thomas S. Monson, Russell M. Nelson, Dallin H. Oaks.

<u>**Aggression**</u>: hostile or violent behavior or attitude toward another; readiness to attack or confront. Chimps, wolves, and red deer are especially aggressive, may even kill or fight to the death. Bonobos are peaceful and cooperative, chimps are aggressive and competitive.

<u>**Agincourt,**</u> battle of: 1415, fought in northern France as a part of the Hundred Years War in which the English under Henry 5th defeated a large French army using long bows, allowed Henry to occupy Normandy.

<u>**Alaska**</u>: US's northernmost state, purchased from Russia in 1867 for about seven cents an acre.

<u>**Alexandria**</u>: city in northern Africa, northwest of Cairo, Egypt, founded in 332 BC by Alexander the Great. Was a Greek city; after destruction of Jerusalem in 70 AD thousands of Jews migrated to Alexandria, where they were "Hellenized." Seventy-two scholars who knew both languages, Greek and Hebrew, translated the Old Testament into the Septuagint in 132 AD. Fell to Muslim conquerors in 646 AD. Today its population is 4.5 million.

<u>**Alienation**</u>: a term used by Karl Marx to describe the deep separation that workers seemed to experience between their innermost sense of identity and the labor

they were forced to perform in order to earn enough money to live. Similar to being robotized, earning money to buy fuel to drive to work to get money to buy more fuel to continue to get to work to get more money in a repeating cycle.

Altruism: unselfish interest in the welfare of others. "He has a reputation as a cunning and cutthroat businessman, but he has also been lauded for his generosity and altruism."

Ambition: a strong desire to do something typically requiring determination and hard work. Also suggests a strong desire for rank or fame. "She was ambitious to become president."

Anachronism: chronologically out of place, especially from a former age that is incongruent in the present. "Manual typewriters and horse-drawn carts are often regarded as anachronistic in the age of computers."

Analyze: to break ideas apart into components, evaluate, deconstruct, parse, disambiguate, dig down.

Anticipatory obedience: a sign of fervent followers who anticipate what the leader wants and they go even further.

Anti-Intellectualism: hostility and mistrust of intellect and intellectuals. Commonly expressed as ignoring altogether or the deprecation of reading, philosophy, education and the dismissal of art, literature, and science as difficult, impractical, scary, abstract, and contemptible.

Anti-Nephi-Lehi: "Those who had not been converted and had not taken upon them the name of Anit-Nephi-Lehi, were stirred up to anger against their brethren. The

Anti-Nephi-Lehi's took their swords, and all the weapons which were used for the shedding of man's blood, and they did bury them up deep in the earth. Rather than shed the blood of their brethren they would give up their own lives; and rather than take away from a brother they would give unto him (in wisdom and order); and rather than spend their days in idleness they would labor abundantly with their hands" (Alma 24:1, 18).

Antinomy: paradoxes from Kant; thesis, antithesis, synthesis, e.g., being, non-being, becoming, e.g., "In a self-existent uncreated universe, created perspectives in their infinitudes have their simultaneous beginning and ending in eternity." "All contradictions and the sum of contradictions have their antinomies."

Anti-Semitism 500 AD to 1306 AD: mainly economic because Jews were stereotypically in finance, lending money, but religious differences were given edge to cover the economic rivalries. The masses did not think to view as unchristian and unjust the holding of an entire people responsible for the sins of a tiny minority of Jews in Jerusalem.

Americans for Prosperity: a political PAC funded mainly by the Koch brothers, Mercer family, DeVos.

Anger: to be mad. "Whoso is angry with his brother shall be in danger of hellfire." "Who the gods would destroy they make angry."

Arab: children of Abraham, especially descendants of Haggar, many are followers of Islam.

Analysis paralysis: weighing the pro and con and investigating every detail so much that no decision is reached, no direction is taken.

Anthropology: The study of human nature, human society, and the human past. EB Taylor was one of the founders of anthropology in Britain.

ASPD: anti-social personality disorder. Also called psychopathy or sociopathy. Not to be confused in individuals with lack of education, general ill-will, evil heartedness, willful selfishness, greed, or using people in the name of thrill seeking. ASPD is a pervasive pattern of disregard for and violation of the rights of others, manifesting itself around age 15. Diagnosed as deficient brain constructs such as small amygdala, failure to conform to social norms, deceitfulness as indicated by lying or conning others for profit, irritability and aggressiveness as indicated by fights or assaults and reckless disregard for the safety of others.

Augustine: not to be confused with Saint Augustine of Hippo who wrote *The City of God*. The Pope sent this Augustine, a Sicilian abbot, to Kent to declare Christianity to the heathen. He arrived in 597 AD, baptized many people, and became the archbishop of Canterbury.

Autocracy: a system of government in which power is concentrated in the hands of one person, whose decisions are subject to neither external legal restraints nor regulated mechanisms of popular control (excepting the implicit threat of coup d'état or mass insurrection). Monarchy and dictatorship are the main historical forms of autocracy.

<u>Augean stables</u>: a condition or place marked by great accumulation of filth or corruption. Based on myth of Augeas, who kept great stables holding 3,000 oxen that had not been cleaned for 30 years. Hercules was assigned the job and diverted two rivers to run through the stables.

<u>Autumn</u>: the season following summer and preceding winter on the northern hemisphere; the close or ending.

B-

<u>Believe</u>, the will to: Durant (1950), in times of poverty and chaos, religion springs to the fore as the only real thing and is paramount to survival and so the emotions dominate; courage is the one needful thing. In ages of wealth the intellectual powers come to the fore. As such, a civilization passing from poverty to wealth tends to develop a struggle between "reason" and "emotion." If holiness triumphs destruction is abated.

<u>Beowulf</u>: legend written around 1000 AD. Beowulf tore off the monster Grendel's arm with his own bare hands.

<u>Bering Strait</u>: named after Vitus Bering (1681 AD to 1741 AD) a Danish sailor, joined the Russian navy to explore the passage between Siberia and America.

<u>Best of All Possible Worlds</u>: Leibniz and Voltaire explore the idea that all is for the best. Since the world was created by a perfect God, everything is just as it should be—the world is perfect the way it is because it was made by a perfectly just God.

Better Angels of our Nature: an Abraham Lincoln quote, "We are not enemies, but friends, we must not be enemies. Though passion may have strained, it must not break our bonds of affection. The mystic chords of memory will harmonize when touched by the better angels of our nature."

Bias: prejudices. Confirmation bias—one looks for information to substantiate already held beliefs; Conviction bias—one believes so strongly that it will make it true; negative bias, positive bias, better than average biases all shape one's outlook and behavior.

Biden presidency, cabinet and other leaders (2021):
        President: Joe Biden
        Vice president: Kamala Harris
        Chief of staff: Ron Klain
        Press secretary: Jen Psaki
        Secretary of State: Anthony Blinken
        Secretary of Defense: Lloyd Austin
        Dept. of Justice: Merritt Garland
        FBI: Christopher Wray
        Homeland Security: Alejandro Mayorkos
        Health: Xavier Becarra
        Housing: Marcia Fudge
        Labor: Marty Walsh
        CIA: David Cohen, William Burks
        National Intelligence: Averil Haines
        International Intelligence: Averil Haines
        Education: Miguel Caradonna
        Interior: Deb Haaland
        Agriculture: Tom Vilsak
        Energy: Jennifer Granholm
        Commerce: Gina Raimondo

Treasury: Janet Yellin
FEMA: Deann Criswell
Consumer Pro: Rohit Chopra
UN: Linda T. Greenfield
Health: Rochelle Wilensky
Surgeon General: Vivek Murthy
Trade: Kathryn Tai
Economic Advisors: Cecilia Rouse, Jared
Bernstein
SEC: Gary Gensler
EPA: Michael Regan

<u>Bigotry</u>: to regard members of a group with hatred and intolerance; prejudice; racism. "There is nothing more dangerous than the conscience of a bigot." There is nothing more destructive than being led by a false spirit under the delusion that it is a true spirit.

<u>Billiards</u>: Leibniz makes the point that apparent forces may not be what they seem. For example, two billiard balls might appear at the atomic level to be colliding; one ball moves the other when they seem to meet in contct. But there may be invisible or unknown forces that cause one ball to stop right before it touches the other ball. Only coincidentally did it move, and that by another totally different force or set of forces that had nothing to do with what appeared to be contact or physical collision. Therefore, our perception of cause and effect might be entirely unjustified (see TESURM). Similar to Zeno's paradox of motion with Achilles and the turtle, making the point that numbers are not space, and space is not moving matter, or mind. They are not identical properties. Numbers, for example, are of a different dimension of matter than what Karl Popper would call "world one" levels of matter found in tables, chairs, light waves, paper, trees, and screens.

Bread and circuses: phrase used by Augustus Caesar and later by Marcus Aurelius. Plebeians were given government subsidized low-priced bread and circuses to keep them from rebelling.

Buddhism: Gautama Siddhartha lived in India around 600 BC, known as the Buddha. Illusion and desire are the cause of suffering; nirvana a condition purported to be free from illusion and desire.

Burke, Edmund: (1729 to 1797) dad/mom/kids family the basis of the social order.

C-

Calvin, John: (1509 to 1564) Atoning grace of Christ was for those elected by their good works to be God's children. The naked deformity of their lives will be covered by charity. All others will be exposed to the full extent of the laws of justice: everything they did and thought and why they did it will be open for all to view, a twisted monstrosity of vanity, cowardice, carnality, and envy.

Capitalism: an economic system dominated by supply and demand, the free market. A way of organizing society that favors the economic activity of private citizens as opposed to socialism or communism where the flow of money is directed more by a few individuals in government.

Capital punishment: the killing of a criminal within a political community after a trial and sentencing in a law court.

Carnegie, Dale: wrote *How to Win Friends and Influence People*. Become genuinely interested, smile, remember names, be a good listener and do not interrupt too soon, talk in terms of other's interests, make others feel important, give honest appreciation and compliment sincerely, let others save face or not be embarrassed, and try to understand their point of view.

Carthage: a city in ancient Africa with an excellent sheltered harbor; and a city in present day Illinois where Gazelem the prophet's blood was shed.

Chaos: is not freedom. Following whimsy, selfishness, lust, greed, and foolishness is not conducive to social order. It leads to disarray, degeneracy, and decay. War, gun control, immorality, abortion, drugs, etc., which cause chaos, are confused with "material freedoms" or "basic rights" when, again, in reality manipulating these emblems may simply be chaos masquerading as will-to-power or "freedom" in the form of rebellion.

Charity: not to be confused with a government dole. A dole is giving something for nothing, which is evil. "Kindness and long-suffering never fail. But whether there be prophecies, they shall ultimately be worth little, just knowing the future isn't going to make you better; whether there be understanding of languages, they will be replaced with better higher means of communication in other worlds; whether there be partial knowledge, it shall come to almost nothing in this world. The things that matter most now and in eternity are faith, hope, and charity; the greatest is charity or pure love" (Corinthians

13). "Without kindness, improvement, and action—without charity ye are nothing" (Moroni 7).

Charlemagne: (742 AD to 814 AD) was king of France, then Roman Emperor as Charles 1st.

Charybdis: pronounced kuh RIB duss. Greek mythology; a dangerous whirlpool opposite the cave of Scylla. The same as being caught between the devil and the deep blue sea or being caught between a rock and hard place. "He was trapped between Scylla and Charybdis with no easy way out."

Celebrity worship: young people look for examples to imitate, heroes. When someone is admired, they may be exalted in other's minds and faults may be overlooked.

Certainty: "Science is an orderly arrangement of what, at the moment, appears to be facts." On a continuum the Changeless Now of All Knowledge may be the most and only really certain thing; at the other side of the continuum is uncertainty and doubt. Pontius Pilate did not heed the following dictum: "Doubt your doubts before you doubt your faith in sacrificing all earthy things to God." From a mortal human point of view, the future is an uncertain thing. Hume points out the *more* a thing happens the *less* likely it is to happen again, such as the sun rising or chickens getting fed. Trump and Biden are not what they used to be. "The future is not what it used to be." Furthermore, the past is not reliably known. The past is an ever-fading Polaroid snapshot, but we go still further into now and see that the immediate present is as much a mystery as anything else. In terms of politics, acting and pretending to be confident or to focus on "certainties" can have a positive effect on voter turnout.

<u>Colonialism</u>: often involves cultural domination with enforced social change in which the weaker group is overtaken by a stronger group. At the macro level entire countries may be affected; at the micro level, say within a company, only one individual may for better or worse feel the effects of being colonized or "bossed around." The British have colonized India, South Africa, and Botswana.

<u>"Conservative" thinkers</u>:

Xunzi: (3rd Century BC) lived in China, thought humans became evil as they gave way to temptation around the age of 16, observed that bodily satisfaction and social prestige dominated behavior. Selfishness is the dark path to misery.

Chanakya: (4th Century BC, 1700 years before Machiavelli) lived in India, believed people are competitive, some self-interest behind friendship. Therefore, we should use some duplicity in our statecraft.

Hobbes: (1588 to 1674) lived in England, believed that in a state of wild nature, life would be relatively solitary, poor, nasty, brutish, and short. Social contracts give power to sovereign to centralize the leviathan to keep peace.

John Locke: (1632 to 1702) believed the mind is a blank slate at birth and sense data writes upon it; people born as innocent victims of freedom. Rulers had no "divine right" to rule but with a social contract people could delegate their power to a ruler to act in their behalf. Natural rights and laws: life, liberty, health, property.

John Stuart Mill: (1806 to 1873) wrote *On Liberty* about utilitarianism, which involves doing the most good for the most people. The most efficient way is not always the best way, but usually it is. Balancing authority and freedom: "If humans were good angels, no formalized government would be necessary. If holy angels were to govern humans, neither external nor internal controls would be necessary. As it is with fallen man, the government must control itself."

Karl Marx: (1818 to 1883) believed human nature is empty and social environments should be arranged so that they become cooperative, working together first through socialism and finally through communism. "From each is taken according to his ability, to each is given according to his needs."

CREEGS: the condition or state of the following properties blended into one property: **c**leanliness, **r**ighteousness, **e**xcellence, **e**ffectiveness, **g**oodness, **s**ervice. "His credence and creegs were on par with the credentials of other qualified individuals." American creegs are what keep us from sinking in a sea of filth and rebellion.

Cultures: sets of learned behaviors and ideas humans acquire as members of a society; the social-environment side of heredity and freedom; the nurture side of nature. Cultures are learned and patterned, traditions. Overcoming foolish tradition is the goal of all honest societies.

Curiosity: to wonder or be inquisitive. Perceptual curiosity involves seeking thrills relating to the five senses; epistemic curiosity involves desire for knowledge about everything including how knowledge itself works; empathic curiosity involves seeking to know how others feel.

D-

Daoism: from the Tao-te Ching. Live simply, honestly, and in harmony with nature.

Defense mechanisms: in psychology (could be compared to military defense) a fancy technical vocabulary has been developed to talk about ways people handle unpleasant possibilities and realities. *Denial* (can also be a euphemism for "dishonest" or "sad") is the refusal to accept reality or facts. *Compartmentalizing* is categorizing to justify or the putting of incompatible thoughts into separate categories, such as swindling folks on weekdays but going to church on Sunday.

Regression is found more in kids who revert to silly younger stage behaviors, but adults can manifest regressions to behavior from younger stage behaviors, too. *Acting Out* is the performing of extreme behavior in place of words such as, punching a wall instead of saying, "I'm upset with you." Acting Out can be a "cry for help." It can be the testing of boundaries. *Dissociation* is the losing track of time and separating the body from the mind by use of the imagination to hide from or ignore bad things such as abuse that happened in the past.

Projection is putting one's own thoughts and motives into another person's who does not have the same thoughts and motives as one wishes they did. *Reaction

Formation or action reformation is taking the opposite course from a natural response, can show up as overcompensation such as someone who hates their boss, instead of quitting becomes extra nice to the boss and says this is her favorite job. *Repression* is the putting away of bad memories. *Displacement* is misdirecting of blame or rewards to the wrong targets, such as a teacher taking out her frustrations on her classes at school because of her cat clawing the furniture at home. *Intellectualization* is overemphasis on thinking in place of emotion.

Rationalization is trying to justify something that is wrong or bad, not to be confused with ratiocination. *Undoing* is not apologizing but trying to make up for a mistake in other ways. *Sublimation* is the redirecting of impulses and desires to other targets, for example instead of eating an entire pizza one tries to become the president of the United States. *Compensation* is the counterbalancing of weakness by emphasizing a strength.

Demagogue: a political leader who seeks support by appealing to the desires and prejudices of ordinary people rather than by using rational argument.

E-

Economy: the wealth and resources of a nation or region, especially in terms of production and labor. "A study of economics usually reveals that the best time to buy anything is last year." The best time to plant a tree is ten years ago, the next best time is today.

<u>Enemy of the People</u>: Trump's definition of the news media such as FOX, CNN, and MSNBC.

<u>Energy</u>: these words are the reorganized energy of yesterday's food. Existence is the food of life. (Existence is also the food of death.) We focus on the positive.

<u>Ever-Ever Land</u>:

> Of ever-ever land I speak,
> sweet morons gather round.
> Who does not dare to stand
> or sit may take it lying down,
> for ever-ever land is a place
> that's simple as simple can be
> and was built that way on purpose
> by simple people like we.
> And ever-ever land is a place
> that's measured and safe and known,
> where it's lucky to be unlucky
> and the Hitler lies down with the Kohn.
> But only sameness is normal
> in ever-ever land,
> for a bad cigar is a woman
> but a gland is only a gland.
> Down with the human soul
> and anything else uncanned,
> for everyone carries can openers
> in ever-ever land.
> Down with hell and heaven
> and all the religious fuss.
> Infinity pleased our parents,
> one inch looks good to us.
> Down above all with love
> and everything written in verse
> or that which makes
> some feel more-better
> when all ought to feel less-worse.
>   -ee cummings

Evil: good and evil are polarized or separated from larger annihilating compounds as one or the annihilating compound as One. Good and evil have come among men, and man is free to choose between them and to act for himself, and to learn by experience. Opposites are the foundation of freedom. Freedom gives birth to opposites. All intelligence is independent in the sphere in which God has placed it. It should seem obvious that everyone would choose the good all the time, but the spirit of the wicked one tempts men with evil and clouds their judgments and mental vison. "Nevertheless, they receive not the light by choice. For man is spirit." (D&C 93).

Evolution: time could be thought of as the abstraction of movement, movement the abstraction of matter, matter an extraction of Mind, and soul an extraction of the Transcendently Changeless Celestial Mind or Spirit—the great I AM, All Knowledge, the Spirit of Truth.

All truth and intelligence is independent in the sphere in which God has placed it to act for itself, otherwise there is no existence. There is no naked time or pure empty space; matter and movement are separated (and combined) within the Endless. The elements are eternal, and there have always been humans on fallen grossified planets like Earth. Spirit and element inseparably connected receive a fullness. Big Bangs and Primeval Eggs and black holes are merely little portions of relativity, of endless matter which can have no center or circumference. The contingent is inside or subordinate to the Necessary; the body is in the mind; the relative is a small portion of the Absolute. Evolution or creation is subordinate to the Sum of Existence. God is in the bosom of Eternity. Relative to ETERNITY, as Moses said, man is nothing. Your life is the sum of your thoughts; your life is your own eternity. Darwinian evolution involves the survival of the fittest, "the management of the creature."

F-

Fair weather friends: a comparison suggesting when the weather becomes unpleasant, or times get difficult the "friend" is no longer there. Generally, a hypocritical position to take.

Fall: move downward from a higher to a lower level; autumn.

Fascism: an authoritarian and nationalistic system of government and social organization. Mussolini of Italy (1922 to 1943) is a prototype of fascism, Hitler of Germany, Franco of Spain.

Fashion: goes in one year and out the other.

Fear: people will look back at the end of their lives to see that fear and money were the major motivations for almost everything they did.

Fiction: sometimes reveals truths that reality obscures.

Freedom: is not chaos. "Men must use their freedom to stop chaos."

FRICAW: pronounced FRY ka. The composite or unity of the following attributes: facts, reality, impartiality, compassion, action, and wisdom. "Perfect fricaw is the means to all good endeavors."

Fusion, cold: nuclear reaction at room temperature.

G-

Gadianton robbers: experts in wickedness. Gadianton became the leader of the band of Kishkumen, unknown by government therefore not destroyed.

Gain: riches, wealth, profit, business. People are often tempted to turn gain into an idol or the object of their worship, effort, and affection.

Gazelem: the Lord will prepare unto his servant Gazelem a stone (Alma 37:23).

God: everlasting Being whose attributes are knowledge, power, justice, judgement, mercy, and truth. "Then shall they confess, who live without God in the world, that the judgment of an everlasting punishment is just upon them; and they shall quake, and tremble, and shrink beneath the glance of his all-searching eye" (Mosiah 27:31).

Googol: 10 to the 100th power.
1,000,000,000,000,000,000,000,000,000,000,000,0
00,000,000,000,000,000,000,000,000,000,000,000,000,
000,000,000,000,000,000,000,000

H-

Hades: land of death that the mythical or fantasy Greek god Hades ruled, brother of Zeus and Poseidon. Other names: Thanatos, Pluto; sheol, spirit world, underworld, hell/paradise. Part of the "day" of this life. Not to be confused with the Last Judgment and the placing of all things in their orders, the final separation of the wheat from the tares, which could be called heaven and hell. "Men fear heaven more than hell. Heaven is much too good for us, and we must learn by degrees to how to handle the holiness and purity thereof." –Hugh Nibley

Hegemony: authority or influence over others, domination.

Hellenism: (320 BC to 30 BC) time period of the Greeks from Alexander the Great to the defeat of Cleopatra and Mark Anthony by Octavian and the subsequent conquest of Ptolemaic Egypt.

Human nature: debate about whether humans are basically good or bad goes on. Rousseau, Hobbes, Pelagius, Augustine, Calvin, Luther, Boyd K. Packer, Maslow, Carl Rogers, Richard Wrangham. Most argue that people are basically good.

Hyperbole: obvious and intentional exaggeration, extravagant statement or figure of speech not intended to be taken literally. "He lived life in a kind of nether world, in a spotlight of hyperbole, seeing everyone's sins but his own."

I-

Ice Ages: 30,000 to 13,000 BC. Land bridges between Europe and England disappeared in 6500 BC.

<u>Idealism</u>: the philosophical view dating back at least to Plato that *mind* is the ultimate matter and is the essence of human existence.

<u>Ideology</u>: a system of ideas or hopes, especially ones that forms the basis of economic or political theory or policy.

<u>Identity</u>: the physical personage or "phizz;" a sense of self based on the ultimate indestructability of the same matter that has and shall always exist, eternal spirit, will, freedom, agency, heredity, environment, social attachments, names, labels, family, friends, neighborhoods, culture, nation, planet, galaxy, schools, teams, size, shape, wealth, achievements, etc.

<u>Ignorance</u>: lack of knowledge, lack of education, lack of awareness. The meaning of the word is ironically taken to mean "rude" among the ignorant classes of people as in, "He was being 'ignorant' towards his sister," the term being confused with the word "belligerent."

<u>Illusion</u>: a thing that is likely to be wrongly perceived or interpreted by the senses; a deceptive appearance or impression.

<u>Image</u>: book by Daniel Boorstin, *The Image: A Guide to Pseudo-events in America* (1962) is a guide to the art of self-deception, an indictment analyzing contrived events and people that are constructed.

<u>Immature reasoning</u>: "If a little is good then a lot must be great."

<u>Inflation</u>: when you pay $15 for the $10 haircut you used to get for $5 when you had hair. Several stimulus packages, when Trump left and Biden came into office, inflated the value of the dollar. Interest rates were subsequently raised by Jerome Powell (chairman of the federal reserve).

Instinct: an innate, typically fixed pattern of behavior in animals. *The Language Instinct* is a book written by Steven Pinker.

Intelligence, I.Q.: the average is 100, presidential average is 143.

Estimated I.Q.s of presidents:

Grant	120
Monroe	138
Bush, W.	138
Johnson	139
Harding	140
Taylor	140
Buchanan	140
Washington	140
Taft	140
Ford	140
Truman	140
Coolidge	142
Hoover	142
Reagan	142
Bush, H.W.	143
McKinley	143
Trump	143
Polk	143
Nixon	143
Cleveland	144
L. Johnson	144
Eisenhower	145
Harrison	145
Jackson	145
Van Buren	146
Hayes	146

Pierce	147
Tyler	148
Fillmore	149
F. Roosevelt	150
Lincoln	150
Biden	150
Garfield	152
Arthur	152
T. Roosevelt	153
J. Adams	155
Wilson	155
J.Q. Adams	155
Obama	155
Carter	156
Clinton	159
Madison	160 (Bill Gates is about this level)
Kennedy	160
Jefferson	160

Note: There is little correlation between I.Q. and good judgment or wisdom. These, like so many other numbers, may be random. Other types of skills and abilities include emotional intelligence, social intelligence, analytic, creative, musical, spatial, reaction time and speed of decision-making, etc. Intelligence could be defined here as the ability to gather and use information to adapt to one's environment.

Charlie Munger said he would rather make important financial investment decisions with someone who had an I.Q of 130 who estimated their own I.Q. to be 129 than with someone who had an I.Q. of 180 estimating it to be 190.

Interpretation: an explanation or translation; a stylistic representation of a creative work. Criticism is prejudice made plausible.

Inventions:

> Magnetic compass
> Paper (100 AD)
> Gunpowder (900 AD)
> Optical lens (1250)
> Printing press (1450) Gutenberg
> Vaccinations (1776) Jenner
> Steam engine
> Internal combustion engines
> Sewers
> Refrigeration (1850)
> End of slavery (1865)
> Telephone (1876)
> Electricity (1879 lightbulbs) Edison
> Airplane (1903)
> Radio (1906)
> Ford Model T (1908)
> Penicillin (1928) Fleming
> Nuclear energy (1939)
> Semi-conductors
> Personal computer
> Internet

Irrational: not logical or reasonable. In math, a technical kind of number with infinite non-recurring expansion when expressed as a decimal such as pi or the square root of 2.

J-

<u>James, William</u>: (1846 to 1910) American philosopher and psychologist, taught at Harvard. "Sometimes people suppose they are thinking when they are merely rearranging their prejudices." Wrote *Principles of Psychology*. Brother was Henry James the novelist.

<u>Jacobins</u>: members of a democratic club that started in Paris in 1789. They claimed to be for equality but were radical and ruthless against the political groups in wake of the French Revolution. Associated with Robespierre who helped institute the reign of terror in 1793. The name comes from a Dominican building that was called Jacobin.

<u>Johnson, Samuel</u>: (1709 to 1784) created a dictionary. "Great works are performed not by strength but by perseverance."

<u>Jung, Carl</u>: (1875 to 1961) born in Switzerland. Psychology of "unconsciousness," persona, archetypes. Believed people have a religious instinct, a kind of divine DNA. "Things that irritate us about others can lead us to an understanding of ourselves."

K-

<u>Kant, Immanuel</u>: (1724 to 1804) European philosopher who tried to improve our knowledge of metaphysics. Nature is the sum of appearances; appearances are not things in themselves. Treat people as ends in themselves rather than as means. Mind is an active agent with its own properties and laws for transforming, processing, and digesting sense data, turning it into ideas and meanings.

Karma: the force generated by a person's actions held in Hinduism and Buddhism to perpetuate "transmigration" and in its ethical consequences to determine the nature of the person's next life; justice; characteristic spirit that vitalizes someone.

Knowledge: "It is impossible for a man to be saved in ignorance." –D&C 131:6.

Know-Nothing Party: The Republican Party was born in the 1850s and Abraham Lincoln was nominated. The Know-Nothings were absorbed into the Republicans.

L-

Laissez-faire: is a doctrine opposing governmental interference in economic affairs beyond the minimum necessary for the maintenance of peace and property rights. However, leaving regulations to corporations can lead to worse pollution, contamination, monopolies, fads, scams, exploitation, and inequality. The invisible hand of Adam Smith depends on responsible and honest people.

Latin language: emerged from Greek as early as 700 BC and spread with the expansion of the Roman Empire. Its ghost haunts many descendants.

Leadership: transactional leadership appeals to self-interest by giving incentives to employees and creates internal competition. Transformative leadership appeals to team spirit and the idea of leaving no one behind, as in the Marines.

Liberalism, Modus Vivendi: advocated by Locke, Adam Smith, Hayek. They believe in freedom and liberty, property rights and First Amendment rights (religion, speech, press) but little intrusion by government. They are less interventionist at home and abroad, are opposed to social engineering, do not feel obliged to spread democracy or push regime change. They rely on rationality but do not believe in equal opportunity, only equality before the law.

Lincoln, Abraham: usually ranked as the best president, first Republican president, issued Emancipation Proclamation in 1863.

Linnaeus typology: kingdom, phylum, class, order, family, genus, species.

Literacy: an educated person has seriously read the Bible, the Book of Mormon, the Doctrine & Covenants, the Peal of Great Price, the Journal of Discourses, Plato, Kant, Dante, Hegel, Locke, Shaw, Mencken, Saint-Exupery, selected Shakespeare, Twain, Keynes, Pinker, Popper, Suess, Peet, etc.

M-

Madison, James: (1751 to 1836) was the son of a wealthy planter in Virginia, home was Montpelier, close to Jefferson's Monticello. He graduated from Princeton in 1771, was a representative from Virginia to the Continental Congress, attended the Constitutional

Convention in 1787, and was president of the US from 1809 to 1817.

Materialism: the modern-day worship of Mammon. Otherwise, dialectical material is moving matter, atoms.

Matter: all spirit is matter; there is no pure or empty space, there is no immaterial matter.

MIODIO: pronounced my oh dye oh. The quality of **m**agnanimity, **i**ncorruptibility, **o**rder, **d**uty, **i**ntelligence, **o**neness. "My goodness! Her level of miodio is really looking good today." American miodio is on the upswing among certain groups.

Moirai: three mythical Greek goddesses who were responsible for the length of human lives. Clotho, Lachesis, Atropos, spun measured and cut the thread at life's end.

Mormonism: slang term for the Church of Jesus Christ of Latter-day Saints, the gateway to the sum of existence and holiness. Mormon is the name of the last prophet to write to his son Moroni at the end of the Nephite time period.

Muon: elementary particle with greater mass than electrons, classified as a lepton. Interactions: gravity, electromagnetic, weak.

N-

Narcissism: the etymology is from the Greek myth of Narcissus who stared at his reflection until he withered and died. Excessive interest in one's self.

Nation: a group of people that share the same history, culture, language, laws, schools, books, geography, food, leaders, and unity of thought.

Natural man: untrained, uneducated, and wild he is an enemy to God "and has been from the fall of Adam and will be forever and ever unless he yields to the enticings of the Holy Spirit, and puteth off the natural man and becometh a saint through the atonement of Christ the Lord, and becometh as a child, submissive, meek, humble, patient, full of love, willing to submit to all things which the Lord seeth fit to inflict upon him, even as a child submits to his father" (Mosiah 3:19).

O-

Offenbach, Jacques: (1819 to 1880) composed the Tales of Hoffmann, Barcarolle. Was popular in Paris.

Origen: (185 to 253 AD) lived in Alexandria, Egypt, influenced by Clement, believed in a restoration of all things.

Orpheus and Eurydice: Greek myth, Orpheus tries to bring her back from the dead with his enchanting music.

Orthodox: "correct doctrine," standard.

P-

Paradigm: a typical example, pattern, or model. A paradigm shift example in public thought is the Ptolemaic system (earth-centered) changing to the

Copernican system (sun-centered). Another example of a paradigm shift is that the mind is a product of the body, this changing to the view that the spirit is a larger sphere than the mortal body. Inside this spirit sphere the body has its limits and boundaries. The body veils the light of knowledge reducing perfect knowledge into, technically speaking, a kind of faith or work or action-of-the-mind which gropes blindly through Leibnizian laws, seemings, giving rise to this system of experience within the great whole of EXPERIENCE, and proving the soul, to see what it will do in the dark.

Pastiche: a hodgepodge, mixture, imitation.

Patriotism: love of one's country. "Patriotism is often the arbitrary veneration of real estate over principles." - George J. Nathan

Popper, Karl: (1902 to 1994) the paradox of tolerance states that if a society is tolerant without limit, its ability to be tolerant is eventually seized or destroyed by the intolerant. Popper described it as the seemingly paradoxical idea that in order to maintain a tolerant society, the society must be intolerant of intolerance.

Power: "Nearly all men can stand adversity, but if you want to test a man's character give him power." – Abraham Lincoln

Prepare: "It is better to prepare and prevent than to repair and repent."

Prescriptive: prescriptivism tells how a thing should be done; it prescribes. Conversely, a descriptivist describes how it is done; for example, a descriptivist grammarian will write like Mark Twain in *Huck Finn,* spelling and characterizing dialogue as it is pronounced by an area's inhabitants.

Public education: "If you think education is expensive, try ignorance," said Thomas Jefferson. The school system is like a pair of one-size-fits-all mental and intellectual underpants issued by a salaried classroom manager and used to support the fashion of ideas in a given time and place. "A child educated only at school is not an educated child," said Victor Hugo. "I never let my schooling interfere with my education," said Mark Twain.

Puritanism: the word "Puritan" was first coined in the 1560s as a derisive term for those who advocated more purity in worship and doctrine. Their rise was directly related to the increased knowledge that came to people in the so-called Age of Enlightenment as people learned to read and write, and as the Bible became more accessible to commoners, many began to read the Bible for themselves. They saw Hellenized Christianity, the devil's old lady, giving birth to spiritually illegitimate children, having an appearance of godliness but denying the power or spiritual content thereof. The salt had lost its savor; miracles and gifts of the spirit had long since died with the proper authority to act in behalf of God until Joseph Smith restored the Church in 1830.

Q-

Quixotic: Foolishly impractical, especially in pursuit of ideals; capricious, unpredictable. Don Quixote is a picaresque or roguish figure. "Trump and Biden had their quixotic moments."

Quakers: started by George Fox (1624 to 1691) and grew out of the Puritan movement in England.

R-

Racism: bad feelings based on racial surface appearances. "The meaning of the word racism consolidates as an unfriendly act by any white man against any non-white man." –Bill Buckley

Risk: chance of loss, hazard. "If you take no risks, you will suffer no defeats. But if you take no risks, you win no victories." –Richard M. Nixon

Roe v. Wade: (1973) legalized abortion.

Rorty, Richard: "National self-respect is a necessary condition for improvement."

Russell M. Nelson: (2020) a seer; president of the Church of Jesus Christ of Latter-Day Saints, the only true and living church on the face of the earth today.

S-

Sanctify: to make holy or purify.

Sanity: "When we realize we are all mad, the mysteries disappear and this world stands explained." –Twain "But I don't want to go among mad people," said Alice. "You can't help it. We are all mad here. I am mad. You are mad." –Carroll

T-

Tabula rasa: the mind in its hypothetical primary blank or empty state before receiving outside impressions or empirical data.

TECHIE: pronounced Tek ee. The quality of temperance, endurance, chastity, health, integrity, esteem. "The computer technician, who liked cultivating chia pets, was working on his techie and also his bird watching skills." American techie is also improving among particular classes.

TESURM: time equals stimulus unto response matrix. He was being tested in a tesurm and found it to be quite challenging. Nevertheless, he wanted to respond properly to the constant and ever-changing flow of stimulus that constituted his life. He wanted to act properly.

Trump's successes: could be taken as an academic exercise in relativity and point of view; met chairman Kim Jung Un in Singapore; preserved Crimean sanctions against Russia; military campaign against ISIS; tax cuts helped corporations and the wealthy.

Tyranny of the majority: the term was suggested by Seneca in ancient Rome and developed more by John Stuart Mill and Alexis de Tocqueville. Might makes right.

U-

<u>Unconditional self-acceptance</u>: the refusal to hurt one's self and others in the present because one has hurt one's self and others in the past. Ceasing negative thoughts and feelings. Here the word "unconditional" means wise, and the word "self-acceptance" means attitude.

V-

<u>Validation</u>: being present, reflection on other's condition, historical context, recognizing reactions, genuineness.

<u>Voltaire</u>: (1694 to 1778) wrote *Candide*. Quotes: "Common sense is not so common." "Don't let good become the enemy of best." "It is forbidden to kill; therefore, all murderers are punished unless they kill in large numbers and to the sound of trumpets."

W-

<u>"W"</u>: George W. Bush, 43rd president of the US, instigated No Child Left Behind testing movement in schools; was in office when airplanes were flown into the Twin Towers of World Trade Center in New York (9/11/2001); and during the economic crash of 2008.

<u>Wall</u>: "And this city became an exceeding stronghold ever after; and in this city they did guard the prisoners of the Lamanites; yea, even within a wall which they had caused them to build with their own hands. Now Moroni was compelled to cause the Lamanites to labor, because it was easy to guard them while at their labor; and he desired all his forces when he should make an attack upon the Lamanites" (Alma 53:5).

War: armed hostile conflict; a state of hostility, conflict, or antagonism. Darwinian natural selection, social Darwinism, survival of the fittest. "Men are drawn by devils to war as a moth to flame." "War gives purpose to soldiers' lives."

War, WW 1: (1914 to 1918) was called the Great War, and "The War to End All Wars." Britain and France fought Germany, much of it in trenches with little movement and no progress. About 20,000,000 were killed plus another 20,000,000 were killed by a world-wide epidemic of Spanish Flu.

War, WW 2: (1939 to 1945) was between Germany, Italy, Japan and France, Britain, US after 1941 when Japan bombed Pearl Harbor. About 60,000,000 killed.

Whitehead, Alfred N.: "We live in details, but we speak in generalities."

Winter: "Now is the winter of our discontent." "Blow thou winter wind, thou art not so cold as mankind's ingratitude." "People don't notice whether it is winter or summer when they are happy."

X-

X-ray: 24th letter of the military alphabet.

Xenophanes: Greek writer who lived in 5th century BC. "It takes a wise man to recognize a wise man."

Y-

Yankee: 25th letter of the military alphabet.

Yorck, Paul: (1835 to 1897) largely unknown German philosopher, purported to have influenced Heidegger. Memories and writings of history are not the same as being alive; feeling, willing, cognizing.

Z-

Zemnarihah: "May the Lord preserve his people in righteousness and in holiness of heart, that they may cause to be felled to the earth all who shall seek to slay them because of power and secret combinations, even as this man, Zemnarihah, hath been felled to the earth" (3 Nephi 4:29).

Zoroastrianism: a religion in Persia about 2000 BC perhaps founded by Zoroaster or Zarathustra. Ahura Mazda is Lord Wisdom, First Cause. A war of good versus evil is underway. In a spiritual war, there will be casualties and losses.

—

Section 2

Commentary

-

Causing millions of prayers to ascend on high for fear of nuclear war with North Korea, many would say Trump started his presidency quite well. As his time came to an end, however, he did not turn people away from attempting to worship him. That cost a few human lives, sacrifices, that Trump seemed willing to make. This burden of regret could have been better, but it could have been worse.

Like Abraham Lincoln, with malice toward none and with charity for all, we pray the God of All Things to forgive us as we repent and improve, to deliver us from our own past sins. We pray the God of fricaw (facts, reality, impartiality, compassion, action, and wisdom) to help us to act more wisely, to move forward with an emphasis on "prepare and prevent" over "repair and repent." Trump and Biden will pray for the same, as conditions, forcing them of their own free wills, begin to prevail in the relatively distant future.

"It is better to prepare and prevent than to repair and repent," as Trump and Biden will say when their heredity, environment, and freedom of will come to order.

By checking the rampant flow of drugs, Trump potentially saved many lives. He slowed minority rebellion that may have increased during Biden's time. Preaching and sometimes implying the doctrine of the dole, giving something for nothing, damaged the country as a whole.

Trump reduced taxes for the rich, causing many to be grateful for their fortunate circumstances. The startling simplicity of his materialistic approach to engaging the executive branch of the government, however, created friction in the FBI and military. Biden's permissive attitude stirred as much trouble as Trump did, but the people managed as best they could to keep the proper attitude. Reminded of the Anti-Nephi-Lehi's in the Book of Mormon, they buried their metaphorical weapons of war.

In the beginning, it was tempting to hope for a slice of the materialistic pie that Trump seemed to believe in so much. Their presidencies were overtaken by the spirit of evil to ever darker degrees. Trump was overtaken by a greater lust for power, undercut by his spiritual weaknesses, and turned away from seeking the help of the Holy Ghost. The outcome resulted in his and the Republican's fall. Like Amlici in the Book of Mormon, he gave way to the things of evil. Biden did the same. But they can repent.

Mentally and physically, what could have been different? Hindsight shows the hot winds of the summer of July 2020 blowing Trump and Biden through the Covid-19 pandemic. $1200 stimulus checks had been sent to the people. The stock market was down; some were profiting enormously for having seen the market drop coming. Others were in a depression. Regardless of the bad news peaches, apples, and plums ripened on trees as usual that summer of 2020. Business sputtered along, spaced and outpaced by the effects of Covid, supply chain shortages, and the government's response to close businesses and schools. As the hot months passed, masks were donned in unairconditioned buildings. Hospitals were pressed to save the lives of suffocating Covid patients. Ventilators, for what they were worth, were in short supply. Kids trick-or-treated as Halloween passed by. November 3rd, 2020, Joe Biden was elected president by a reasonable margin—after the storming of the Capitol building—two months later on January 6th. Trump supporters broke into the building and interrupted a joint session of Congress gathered for the counting of electoral votes, causing Speaker of the House Nancy Pelosi and other assembled law makers to hide under tables while security guards drew guns to keep back potential attackers who stormed the premises.

In themselves, the people realized that the process of perfecting fricaw (facts, reality, impartiality, compassion, action, and wisdom) continued in the storms and in the calm. Even under these circumstances, rather than stirring up devilish contention, Trump's fans were mostly conservative citizens who favored limited government, low taxes, limited regulations, free market capitalism, and supported business and free enterprise. The media worshipped such spectacle and the money it generated through advertising revenues.

Even the Trump worshiper in his heart appreciated durable institutions, bold scapegoats, strong military and defense, and conservative church. They stereotypically supported gun rights, open carry and assault rifles for family, fun, and freedom; supported the 2nd Amendment (right to bear arms); and supported the

NRA. Furthermore, stereotypically speaking, Trump fans supported the 1st Amendment (freedom of religion, speech, press, assembly, and the right to petition for redress of grievances); and they seemed to believe in the US Constitution and Bill of Rights, considered to be divinely inspired. Later, in terms of free speech after Biden was elected, Trump filed a lawsuit against Facebook and Twitter for banning his accounts. In January 2024, Trump was sued by columnist E. Jean Carroll, $83 million for defamation.

Trump supporters purported self-reliance and tried to create jobs for the poor; they were careful to not encourage or support freeloaders and avoided dependence on others including the government. They knew there was an inverse relationship between reliance on the State and reliance on self.

Citizens were affected by the generations who were raised on the dole, by white-collar drug dealers, excessive immigration and the negative side-effects of multiculturalism, automation, and globalism. Plato would remind them that too many doctors and lawyers is a sign of a diseased society.

If there were any efforts on the part of Biden or Trump to unify America under God, they were appreciated by citizens, to purify their hearts without hypocrisy, with liberty and justice for all. And, like Thomas Jefferson, they trembled for their country when they reflected that God is a God of justice.

Election, January 2021

Joe Biden and Kamala Harris received 81,000,000 votes, 52% and 232 electoral votes. Trump and Pence received 74,000,000 votes, 48% with 174 electoral votes; the election was certified on January 2021. For many voters in the case of Trump's fall / Biden's autumn, they were caught between the devil and the deep blue sea.

Those in favor of Joe Biden may have seen him as older but wiser, more decent and fair-minded, though he leaned toward a dark permissivism which they hoped would be a better choice than the war-like peace-promoting heavy-handed laisse-faire of Trump.

Trump may have been viewed as a brave, fiery-tongued narcissist driven to violence by a will to unrighteous dominion and a lust for power. Testing the waters as to what he might get away with, Trump struggled to manage the fall and charged the election as illegally stolen by fraud. His attorneys tested the vote count accuracy in many states, but no fraud or other substantial irregularities were found by any courts. He was convicted in the state of Georgia in 2023 for unlawfully conspiring to change the election outcome while participating in a criminal enterprise. Trump's base of fifty million republican voters were upset, some hoping that he was called of God. In 2024, a Colorado group attempted to bar Trump from running for the presidency a second time, based on the 14th Amendment, on grounds of supporting an insurrection.

Robbed

In recent years and compared to Japan, America became increasingly multicultural. Lots of immigrants came to find freedom, jobs, healthcare, and a better life. But millions of Americans struggled to control emotions connected to differences with people of different colors, with those who were uneducated, and with the objectively foolish. The struggle with the burden-causer and those who abode irrational belief systems could have been mitigated had people looked at their own sins rather than at their neighbors.

For their part, it was difficult for immigrants to assimilate to a new culture. Climbing up is more difficult than falling down. The amount of work, effort, time, energy, will, and cost to rise to higher heights was overwhelming for the first generation of immigrants. Take the following example: in France, Muslims from Algeria were having a difficult time fitting into French culture that is Catholic and quite anti-Muslim. Mexicans who moved to Japan in select cases were documented to have quite a hard time adjusting to a more orderly and demure structure of life. In the US, millions of good jobs were lost to automation or were outsourced to other countries such as Mexico, China, and India where wages were lower. Globalization kept prices low on imported goods and helped workers abroad but not for workers in the USA. As a result, workers' wages stagnated since about 1970 if adjusted for inflation.

In his time, Donald Trump slowed illegal immigration but allegedly, in one instance, had some effect on separating about 600 children from their parents; Trump's department of Justice encouraged

Homeland Security to carry out the separation of illegal kids and parents as needed.

Furthermore, Trump did not encourage CEOs, the rich, and wealth holders to do themselves justice by increasing the wages of their hirelings. A small minority were extremely wealthy in 2020 with big increases of millionaires and billionaires. High tech geniuses, such as Jeff Bezos, Bill Gates, the deceased Steve Jobs, and many in banking and real estate were incredibly rich, and some did do themselves justice by paying fair wages. The well-educated elite including doctors, accountants, scientists, and business owners who earned upper middle-class incomes usually ranging from $100,000 to $500,000 per year did justice to the poor in some cases. These experts also had good benefits packages including health and life insurance, company contributions to their retirements, and quite good job security.

Meanwhile, the working class endured stagnant salaries, limited benefits packages, and they were more vulnerable to layoffs during hard times. They might have felt threatened by people who seem different, such as immigrants, Muslims, and others of different colors, religions, and political parties. These were competing for employment. When Trump was elected in 2016, many workers were hopeful for changes that would improve conditions for them. These improvements were what Trump voters were drawn to and continued to hope for and rally around, even after the election was over.

Freedom is Not Chaos

Looking back at the work, bravery, shock, and entertainment provided by Trump with his overconfident charisma, we saw that he was a genius at dominating the media every day. The personification of bread and circuses, he provided comfort and reassurance to citizens who were scared or angry and wanted redress of their grievances— those who wanted vengeance, a target to blame, and who believed conspiracy theories that offered explanations for their troubles.

Anti-family subtleties and anti-mom-in-the-home efforts raged in the lives of many across the world. Abused and neglected kids struggled to become educated, yet many found success. The effort to read in the home was successful. Money was spent on things of infinite value; it was used to help families. In terms of families, nepotism was not one of Trump's weaknesses. Having plenty of family members on the staff and advising him, Trump kept a narrow focus on close relatives as part of his presidency, firing few to none of them. For whatever reasons, their personal tax documents were sought by the media but not displayed publicly. At national levels, he cut taxes for the wealthy, for corporations, and some taxes for average working-class families. He also tried to reduce regulation for business and cut paperwork.

Not wanting degeneracy and minority permissivism to infringe on religious freedom, Trump nominated hundreds of conservative judges including three Supreme Court justices. This was important to religious followers, such as white evangelical Christians and conservative Catholics. Religious freedom would be challenged.

Until Covid-19 hit in early 2020, the national economy did quite well. During Covid, the stock market plunged but gradually recovered and/or stagnated. Businesses and schools were closed, and workers were laid off. There was an emergency rush (Operation Warp Speed) to find effective vaccines, and by the spring of 2021 at least five pharmaceutical companies were supplying millions of doses around the country. In early spring of 2021, unemployment nationally was 7%. Stock markets mostly recovered, and the Dow Jones was about 30,000 a few months later.

Trump, before these events, had engaged peace efforts in the Middle East, moved the US embassy to Jerusalem, slowed ISIS; and decreased business regulation, regulation for emissions, weakened the EPA; and did not get America into a war other than civil strife after the election.

Biden kept on the fringe of the Russia Ukraine and Israel Hamas wars. Senate Majority Leader Chuck Shumer negotiated funding for these in 2024. Interest rates and inflation increased during Biden's time, leveling off around February 2024.

Section 3

Psychological Assessments

-

Pain is not the end of our undertaking. We are doing a great job. But on relative scales of comparison, it pains various souls to acknowledge the following possibilities. Trump, as a nationalist, evoked, aroused, and induced analysis, criticism, and intrigue among psychiatrists who suggested he was a psychopath. At least, they suggested he scored high on the narcissistic personality disorder end of the spectrum. They thought of Trump as selfish, rude, spoiled, and undisciplined, though an eventual student of fricaw, creegs, and miodio.

We can all feel appropriate sorrow. Sensuality is regrettable. The qualities a person must gain in order to obtain and remain in democratic perfection require challenges and battles of all kinds. Americans look for the positive and good and cease to speak evil of others. Americans direct time and money to educating the poor. They are grateful to those who have helped them as kids; they are grateful to those who are helping the poor and the uneducated masses. Parents who are reading together with their kids and strengthening their families are thereby strengthening the nation and the world. Directing funding, money, time, and effort away from foolishness and away from the war machine into helping and educating elementary school kids and parents is not the only way to collective improvement. Nor is selfishness of any use.

Psychologists alleged Trump had weaknesses. They suggested he was narcissistic, unrealistic, and willing to do bad things. Being dishonest, not merely poetic, in terms of delusional disorder involves creating one's own reality, e.g., losing the election being a lie. Psychologists said Trump might have been relatively psychopathic in more ways than one—Trump did not seem to know right from wrong, had no moral compass, and did not seem to care about others—measured even on a brash New Yorker scale of comparison. Whether or not we subscribe whole-heartedly to such terms, Trump's strengths may have become his weaknesses, giving Biden the advantage.

Biden's Advantage

When it came to international relations prior to Biden's election, some US allies may have felt alarmed and offended. Trump visited Putin and Russia and met Kim Jong Un of North Korea. The British floated a large inflatable balloon depicting Trump in a diaper on one of his European tours.

It has been said he short-changed and denigrated public education through Betsy DeVos, Education Secretary, who had no experience in public education but liked private schools; DeVos and Prince families were big donors to Trump (Amway money). Education was not priority number one. For example, he did not propose nursing and jailing facilities be added to public schools for those at the Bell curve extremes, the dysfunctional, the unwilling, and for the severely disabled. He did not push a system that allows students who pass and demonstrate competency to immediately move up to the next level. Trump and Biden could have but did not propose a national school schedule adjustment, one designating time to be used more productively for education, separating useful learning from the daycare and athletics composite mingled in most schools. Such a schedule adjustment might consist of going to school one week on then one week off, year-round, paying parents when their kids get good grades and fining those parents who rank below certain standards. Trump and Biden could have reorganized the education system to include or exclude nursing and jailing facilities for kids who are better suited to abide such conditions. They could have reorganized the system to move qualified competent kids quickly into the workforce.

Trump's conservative judges aided the NRA (national rifle association) and reduced restrictions on gun control. Trump encouraged armed protestors at his rallies which is legal (2nd Amendment) but intimidated other protestors.

Trump encouraged Nationalist Evangelical Christians to be more of a political party than to actually read and really live the teachings of the New Testament, Pearl of Great Price, and the Book of Mormon. Not President Russell M. Nelson the prophet of God, but leaders such as Robert Jeffress and Ralph Reed, were religious and political advisors to Trump.

Trump leaned toward authoritarianism, almost what some would call fascism, by at least not discouraging Proud Boys, Neo-Nazis, militia groups,

Qanon, and southern secessionist rebels. In 2016, Chris Stewart said, "Trump is our Mussolini."

Another advantage given to Biden was Trump's handling of the Covid pandemic; he denied it at first; he would not wear a mask and encouraged followers not to wear masks. Generally speaking, as a result of Covid-19, there was widespread worry: media chaos, conflict, and closed businesses led to extensive cultural anxiety, stress, and sadness, especially among the old and among TV viewers.

Therefore, giving rise to doubt for future leaders and moderate Republicans such as John Curtis and Mitt Romney, Trump's presidency may have generated dissonance for Republicans who supported him, such as Ted Cruz, Josh Hawley, and Lindsey Graham, causing them to backpedal to justify their support for Trump and for the Republican Party of the future. Reaping what is sown, one does not pick apples from thorn bushes. One does not work foolishness without a punishment; one does not work wisdom without a reward.

But again, many good things were accomplished, and we forgive our enemies, let alone our family and friends. What we have felt and what we have known has always shined through what we have shown. We do not label each other in foolishness. And we dub each other forgiven.

Although he knew and privately admitted that he lost the election, Trump convinced himself by reading online protests then created "The Big Lie" that the election was rigged. He protested the election of Biden for two months leading to the Capitol insurrection in DC and underwent impeachment (twice) by the House of Representatives and Senate.

Trump's language, though hyperbolic and expressive, was not always truthful; the Big Lie that he won the election, repeated often enough led millions of his committed worshipers to believe it or act, even if they did not believe. About 8,000 stormed the Capitol, and five died directly or indirectly from the raid.

Delusions are beliefs that are held despite factual evidence to the contrary. Delusions are usually believed with certainty despite their falseness and improbability. They can have a variety of themes including grandeur or persecution. Delusions are usually not of the bizarre sort seen in the movies, such as being poisoned by the CIA, but rather manifest themselves in ordinary figures of speech except that each word is meant literally, e.g., "I alone am the chosen one, invincible, extraordinary beyond words, the very best of the best in everything."

The following is taken from— Lee, Brandy ED. (2018). *The Dangerous Case of Donald Trump*.

1) He believed that the wall would solve many problems for US and Mexico including drugs, sex traffic, terrorists.

2) Believed the CIA while railing against incompetence of the intelligence community.

3) Our culture has become self-centered, "selfies," materialistic, too centered on appearance, bombast, winning at all costs, mindless consumerism, electronic screens, spectacle, and reputation.

4) Trump seemed to admire dictators such as Putin, Kim Jong, Assad, Saddam Hussein. An unopposed dictator can demand adulation and eradicate dissent from all perceived enemies.

5) Delusional people tend to be thin-skinned and humorless regarding their delusions.

6) Delusions are central to the sufferer's existence and questioning them elicits a jolting visceral response.

7) Delusional disorder is chronic, even life-long in some cases and tends to worsen in adulthood.

8) Words and actions are consistent and logical if the basic premise of the delusion is accepted as reality. "Because I am superior to all, it follows that I would never apologize because I am never wrong."

9) General logical reasoning and behavior are unaffected unless they are specifically related to the delusion.

10) The person has a heightened sense of self-reference and trivial events assume outsized importance when they are contradicted.

As we investigate our own perceptions of Biden's Autumn, we should be cautious that the Wittgensteinian "bewitchment of language" does not taint our emotions or interfere with fricaw. Facts must prevail. Reality, impartiality, compassion, action, and wisdom must prevail. We must not become mad, angry, or slothful just because others are planning to do nothing. We must not become inarticulate just because others are muddying the waters of truth.

Anger and fear are not good. We must not become immobile or incoherent in the cause of fricaw. In the end, the great task of the American people is to protect the sacred from the profane.

Section 4

Masses

-

In a book written by Eric Hoffer (the longshoreman philosopher), he describes psychological causes of fanaticism and the nature of mass movements. Hoffer argues that states' goals or values differ, but mass movements are interchangeable, and that adherents will flip from one movement to another. Their motivations are interchangeable. Thus, secular religion, nationalism, and social movements whether radical or reactionary, tend to attract the same type of followers who behave the same way and use the same tactics and rhetorical tools. For example, communism, socialism, Muhammadism, Islam, populism, and white nationalism or black nationalism may attract a variety of "misfits," such as the chronically bored, the physically disabled, the perpetually ill, the talentless, criminals, and sinners.

In all cases, Hoffer argues, these people feel as if their individual lives are meaningless and worthless. There are some particular mass movements that demand a "total surrender of distinct self" (I'll be whatever you want me to be). These identify as a member of a certain tribe or family, whether religious, political, revolutionary, or nationalist. Hoffer identifies this communal sensibility as the key to a "primitive state of being, common among premodern cultures."

Mass movements use play acting and spectacle designed to make the individual feel overwhelmed and awed by their membership in the tribe, as with the massive ceremonial parades and speeches of the Nazis.

Mass movements need not believe in a god, but they must believe in a devil. There must be a common enemy. Hatred or war unifies the group, and the true devil is a foreigner. Jews were Hitler's interloping foreigners who muddied German purity.

Followers of mass movements are usually authoritarian-type personalities, and the leaders are usually dominant right-wing authoritarians. Against such we check ourselves and make sacrifices in order to seek the right things and the right reasons.

Michael Wolfe, a journalist and author, wrote a book entitled *Fire and Fury: A Look Inside the White House*. It sold more than a million copies. Wolfe had firsthand access to Trump and saw the campaign and White House as chaotic, but with staff working hard to control Trump and they did get some work done. Some called Trump a moron and idiot, reporting that he reads little—especially in any depth, watches TV, mostly FOX. He paid little attention in briefings. He sipped as many as 5 diet Cokes on a bad day, had angry tantrums, and had a profane verbal exchange with Mitch McConnell and McConnell would not speak to Trump for weeks.

Perhaps Trump thought that he could charm Putin and others as a great deal maker. He and Hunter Biden may have been compromised in some way with the Russians. Russia's economy is small, about the size of Italy's. So, using cyber warfare was a cheap way to threaten the US, destroy NATO, to get the US out of Syria.

On the weekend of July 16th, 2020, Trump visited NATO, the European Union, Merkle of Germany, Macron of France, and had a visit with the Queen of England.

Anne Applebaum of the Washington Post believed that Trump wanted constant attention and praise, so he suggested Clinton and Obama caused the trouble, that the European Union was a faux puppet. Then he tried to smooth things over by effusive compliments which he hoped would be reciprocated.

Trump maintained that he was a stable genius, and that he had a bigger nuclear button on his desk than North Korea's Kim Jong Un. He implied that the strong stock market and high employment rates were due to him. Market corrections, down-turns, and dips were not due to him. He campaigned frequently, even in late 2021 after Biden had been embroiled in an inflationary economy for months. Trump would continue to hold rallies.

Trump Challenges

Trump had a massive layoff of cabinet and staff in his first year. He fired Gary Cohn as budget director and replaced him with CNBC commentator Larry Kudlow. Kudlow was laissez faire, did not like regulations. Secretary of State Rex Tilerson was replaced by Mike Pompeo, director of the FBI.

Trump was impeached or denunciated twice and acquitted. He said, "We've only just begun to make

America great." The following were impeachment accusations against Trump: he was a racist, liar, and did not pay certain taxes. His tax cuts helped the wealthy and corporations, increased the national debt, created deficits. Tax cuts ballooned the federal deficit to more than $3 trillion. Abuser of women, accused of assaulting 19 women (Reese, Bob and Clifton Jolly. August 18, 2019. "Ten Reasons Republicans should vote Democrat." Tribune.).

Republicans against Trump or GOP for Biden

The following labels may describe who sided with Biden: Many college educated especially with graduate degrees, older people, women, suburban, black women, Mary Trump (niece), George Bush, Rick Wilson, George Conway, John Heinemann, Michael Steele, Jeff Flake, Mitt Romney, McMaster, Coates, Mueller, Collin Powell, Fauci, Jon Huntsman, John Bolton, Karl Rove, John Curtis, Ben Sasse, John Kelly, New York Times "worst president of modern times," Salt Lake Tribune, Scientific American, some European political leaders, California, Hawaii, New Hampshire, Vermont.

Those Who Supported Trump

A list of those who leaned to the Trump side: McCarthy, McConnell, Pompeo, Barr, Cornyn, Jim Jordan, Mike Pence, Reyes, Mike Lee, Bob Oakes, Don Peay, Burgeess Owens, Lou Dobbs, Stuart Varney, Tucker Carlson, Maria Bartiromo, the wealthy, stock owners, businessmen, men more than women, inclement black men, war hawks, strong defense oriented people, Senate Republicans, almost all Republicans, Newt Gingrinch, Chris Christie, Tea Party, Conservative Coalition New York Post, Russians, Putin, Deseret News, Boyd Matheson, Evangelical Christians (78%), white Catholics (52%), Jewish (27%), "rednecks," less educated, authoritarians, those afraid of freeloaders, limited help for needy, those afraid welfare pays more than work, Fox News such as Hannity, Carlton, Varney, Murdoch's, Norquist, Kudlow, Meadows, Mitch McConnell, KKK, right wing militias, Neo-Nazis, Mike Lee, Greg Hughes, Herbert, Reyes, Burgess, Owens, Texas, Montana, Wyoming, Louisiana, John Kennedy, Scalise, John Cornyn, Nunez, Jim Jordan, Mark Maetz of Florida.

Big Money and GOP Contributors

Adelson, Koch, Devos, Princes, Merces, wall street (but seemed to be turning toward Biden because of help for poor, building infrastructure, tax reform, economy), Amy Coney Barrett.

Biden in Office

A year from July 2020, Biden was still alive—a genuine concern for some because he was the oldest president to take office.

Dallin H. Oak's admonition against violence was vindicated.

House Democrats proposed a government-run credit reporting system. A delta variant of Covid-19 spread in India and took a toll on unvaccinated countries. The Dow Jones was around 34,700 and was at 25,800 the year before. Biden's administration ordered a halt on executions, reversed the ban on transgender military personnel, reversed the Muslim travel ban, and put a halt to the Mexico border wall monies.

Russia (Putin) attacked the Ukraine, February 2022. Hamas attacked Israel in October 2023. Inflation rates were as high as they were in the 1980s; banks like First Republic felt the strain, some banks failed. Chairman of the Federal Reserve Jerome "Jay" Powell raised interest rates to about 8%.

Enmity, jealousy, fear, and pride were some of the forces of destruction that eroded the fabric of civility. Good parenting held things together. Helping and improving the family, helping mom and dad, the basic unit of society, should have been Trump's, Biden's, and every American's number one priority. We must make it so now. Good parenting must become our national pastime. Rich Wilson said, "We help kids to help kids." When presidents fail to build up the family, they usher in the winter of our discontent. What Presidents do is out of our control. And so, we take it upon ourselves to build up the family.

www.ingramcontent.com/pod-product-compliance
Lightning Source LLC
Chambersburg PA
CBHW031155250726
48655CB00002B/987